I0454470

Contents

Introduction

Today's Human Resources (HR) significantly differs from its risk-averse origins. The field now embraces progressive practices that are reshaping the HR landscape. Staying updated on HR changes can be challenging, but I'm here to guide you. We'll dispel myths, question conventional wisdom, cultivate a forward-thinking mindset, and explore how to forge a successful, enduring career in the field. This book is not just about HR; it's a redefinition. Whether you're an HR professional, a business leader, or simply curious about the post-pandemic work landscape.

In contrast to past innovations, such as the internet and social media, the rapid evolution of generative AI requires leaders to adapt swiftly. While foreseeing the future is challenging, initiating the journey to understand and leverage generative AI is crucial for transforming the future of work.

Explore the transformative potential of generative AI in recruiting and talent acquisition. Learn how generative AI enhances efficiency, experiences, and outcomes for recruiters, job seekers, and hiring managers. Explore its impact on internal mobility and discover ten crucial questions for vendors using generative AI. Gain insights into the future role evolution of recruiters and hiring managers. Generative AI is a significant game changer in this domain.

Generative AI will revolutionize the future of learning and development (L&D), enhancing instructional design, personalized learning, upskilling, and internal mobility. With Gen AI, measuring learning effectiveness and aligning L&D strategies with business goals becomes more powerful. The aim is to inspire you to envision the possibilities with Gen AI and actively shape the future of L&D. Join the journey to architect the future of learning and development using Gen AI.

Recruiting, fundamentally unchanged for a long time, is now exploring a skills-first approach that evaluates candidates based solely on their ability to perform. This shift is crucial, considering the historical bias in mindset. Past efforts to foster diversity lacked the necessary education, leading to frustration and misunderstandings. Similarly, a skills-based recruiting strategy may face resistance without proper education. To bridge the gap, align DEI goals with recruitment strategies, understand DEI benefits, and educate hiring managers. A skills-first approach is intertwined with DEI, and clarity on goals facilitates effective implementation.

Leverage Generation Z (born 1997 to 2012) as a growth catalyst for your organization by ensuring their sustained engagement. Gen Z acknowledges the prevalence of technology in the workplace and actively adapts to these changes. Recognizing the importance of skill development, they seek a career aligned with their skills. This book explores understanding Gen Z, recognizing their unique motivations compared to previous generations, and aligning their career development with your business's growth.

Employees face the constant challenge of acquiring new knowledge and skills due to the increasing sophistication of tools, machinery, and software. Traditional learning methods struggle to keep pace with these changes. For instance, a worker in a modern plant requires diverse skills such as computer proficiency, problem-solving, diagnostics, machinery operation, and interpersonal communication. The complexity of jobs demands critical thinking, negotiation, problem-solving, and effective communication. Moreover, the growing number of communication channels, including text, email, voicemail, face-to-face meetings, virtual meetings, phone-based apps, and the metaverse, adds another layer of complexity. The current educational and corporate approaches often rely on outdated methods, emphasizing knowledge and task-based instruction. There's a pressing need for a fresh perspective, focusing on skills-based learning that equips employees with flexible, adaptable, and transferable skills for various tasks.

Have you ever undergone a life-changing learning experience? One that profoundly impacted your personal and professional life? Such transformative experiences often exhibit elements of what psychologists call a "state of flow." Imagine being an L&D leader who consistently unlocks the potential of every team member. Your training resonates with individuals, sparking curiosity, continuous learning, and a hunger for professional development. Introducing the INCLUDE model—a simple, practical approach to crafting inclusive learning environments that foster growth for learners of all identities and backgrounds. It's time for learning professionals to embrace the power of inclusive experiences, creating a path for genuine change and development for everyone.

Navigating change in Diversity, Inclusion, and Belonging (DIBs) is a constant in the HR field. Despite evolving terminology and approaches, the intention for positive DIBs practices is common. However, the work can be daunting, and you may feel unsure of where to start. I aim to assist you in strategically consolidating your skills, providing immediate actions, and planning for substantial changes in your DIBs efforts.

Learn how to effectively address non-inclusive behavior by becoming an ally at work. Many struggles with inaction due to fear of mistakes or charge ahead without sufficient reflection. Being an ally means supporting groups to which you don't belong, like a male ally on gender issues or a white ally on race issues. This book provides the tools to confidently act as an ally.

The effectiveness of a skills-first strategy approach relies on utilizing skills data. We will focus on obtaining, defining, measuring, storing, and validating skills, ultimately guiding the development of a data-driven skills-first workforce strategy.

Chapter 1 Redefining HR

Develop a compelling employer brand

Have you ever applied to a company knowing nothing about it? Probably not. More likely, you weren't familiar when you first saw the job posting, but you quickly went into research mode, checking the company's career site, Googling them, and looking at Glassdoor ratings. Congratulations, you've experienced an employer brand. It's the perception of what it's like to work at a company. Every company has one, whether consciously crafted or not. Investing in an employer brand involves creating an employer value proposition (EVP), a statement telling employees what they'll gain from working at the company. It doesn't require a huge budget. Here are four low-cost actions to enhance your employer brand:

1. Invest in compelling job descriptions.

2. Audit your career site and job descriptions for inclusive language.

3. Embrace transparency by acknowledging company faults.

4. Develop an auto-response FAQ email for job applicants to enhance the candidate experience and employer brand.

Write job descriptions that convert

When was the last time a job description evoked genuine feelings in you? Most likely, the answer is rarely. Job descriptions tend to be uninspiring, but that's an opportunity to change. Reflect on your current job description or find a similar one on LinkedIn. Did it truly capture your role or help you envision yourself in that position? Probably not. Here's how to enhance job descriptions and attract more qualified applicants:

1. Consult recent hires in similar roles for insights into why they joined and what they enjoy. Incorporate their perspectives into job descriptions.

2. Write job descriptions for job seekers, using "you" to establish a connection with readers.

3. Eliminate non-essential qualification bullets, focusing on crucial requirements.

4. Optimize for mobile viewing, as most readers access job descriptions on mobile devices. Be concise and efficient with your wording.

5. Enliven job descriptions with hyperlinks, visuals, video, and audio to break up content and make them stand out.

6. Include compensation ranges to improve the efficiency of your applicant funnel.

Remember, job descriptions are crucial employer brand assets, so approach them with creativity and care to elevate their quality.

Optimize your recruiting process

Take a moment to recall your best and worst recruiting experiences. Identify what made the positive ones special and what caused discomfort in the negative ones. Now, conduct an exercise:

1. Draw a vertical line on a piece of paper.

2. List your best candidate experiences on the left side.

3. Document your worst candidate experiences on the right side.

4. Compare your current recruiting process to both lists, identifying gaps between your practices and the best experiences, as well as any practices aligned with the worst experiences.

This exercise serves as a starting point for optimizing your recruiting process. Congratulations on establishing a plan for building better recruiting capabilities.

The importance of mission, vision, and values

Your values are like a compass for your organization, guiding decisions, behavior, and strategy. They shape your employee experience and should be operationalized in three key ways:

1. Incorporate them into your career site: Make values visible for potential applicants, ideally as standalone content.

2. Design values-aligned interview questions: Avoid the outdated concept of "culture fit" and focus on values alignment, using questions like, "Describe the ideal environment where you do your best work."

3. Integrate values into rewards and recognition programs: Ensure they are visible and celebrated to reinforce their importance.

Leadership, especially the CEO and leadership team, plays a crucial role in modeling and reinforcing these values. If not, values risk becoming mere words.

Build a company for everyone

In HR, our crucial role is building inclusive companies that embrace diverse beliefs, backgrounds, ethnicities, orientations, genders, religions, locations, and generations. This responsibility requires individual HR practitioners to prioritize education on diversity, equity, inclusion, and belonging. Success in these efforts hinges on practitioners navigating uncomfortable situations, showing empathy, addressing biases, and recognizing that the journey is ongoing. While building a company for everyone requires executive support and comprehensive programs, individual efforts, though not all-encompassing, contribute significantly.

Master internal communications

In the current communication landscape, with smartphone users receiving 46 push notifications daily and office workers getting 121 emails each workday, attention spans are only 8.25 seconds. Crafting effective internal communications requires strategies to cut through the noise. Here are five tips:

1. Optimize for mobile: Assume your audience reads messages on their phones. Be concise with clear calls to action and efficient copy.

2. Utilize various channels: Engage employees through email, text messages, intranet, video, and preferred channels.

3. Create interactive content: Employ polls, videos, GIFs, and infographics to compete with attention-grabbing platforms like TikTok.

4. Embrace storytelling: Make your message more compelling by conveying it through stories.

5. Leverage artificial intelligence: Enhance your writing with generative AI tools like ChatGPT for a more impactful communication strategy.

Make remote and hybrid work, work

The COVID-19 pandemic rapidly pushed HR into remote work, significantly impacting businesses. While remote and hybrid work became default for many, it's crucial to recognize that not all employees can benefit from it. Today, as companies and employees deliberate on work structures, focusing on remote and hybrid work is essential. HR plays a pivotal role in designing thoughtful, flexible, and adaptive remote and hybrid work programs. Five keys to optimize these models include:

1. Prioritize asynchronous communication to save time.

2. Measure outcomes, not hours, using tools like OKRs.

3. Be intentional about interactions, emphasizing optimized meeting practices.

4. Default to asynchronous communication, making written collaboration the norm.

5. Enhance recognition efforts in the absence of traditional water cooler moments.

Implementing these practices will attract employees seeking work-life balance and flexibility.

Leverage skills to drive talent mobility and retention

The connection between development and retention, many companies overlook the impact of skill development on internal talent mobility. When employees feel they're growing professionally, they're more likely to stay. To foster talent mobility and enhance retention:

1. Identify employees' strengths and capabilities.

2. Invest in their skills through training, mentorship, and education.

3. Implement career ladders and lattices for fluid talent movement.

This approach benefits the company with increased retention, engagement, and cost savings, while providing employees a sense of growth and fulfillment, contributing to a powerful retention strategy.

The keys to successful HR transformation

In recent years, HR has undergone significant transformation due to various factors like COVID, remote work, and social justice issues. Successful HR transformation requires key elements:

1. Leadership Commitment: Obtain commitment from top leadership by aligning transformation efforts with both business and people goals. Emphasize ROI and use business language.

2. Digital Integration: Embrace HR technology, including AI, automation, and data analytics. Apply design thinking to create tailored digital solutions focused on user experience, involving employees in testing.

3. Communication: Clearly communicate the impact of HR transformation at all stages to facilitate understanding and acceptance. Effective communication is vital during change.

4. Employee Experience: Prioritize people in HR transformation. Engage employees in co-creation, involve them in digital strategy meetings, and ensure digital solutions address their actual needs. Constantly ask how initiatives enhance employee productivity, engagement, efficiency, and support.

By incorporating these keys, HR can create an exceptional employee experience that attracts and retains talent.

Build business acumen

Business acumen, a crucial skill for HR professionals, involves understanding and aligning with the organization's strategy, goals, and resources. Neglecting this aspect can limit HR's value and lead to taking on excessive work. Building business acumen enhances both organizational performance and personal career stability.

Here's how to develop this skill:

1. Understand Your Business: Dive deep into your company's products, competitors, and customers. This knowledge empowers you to make informed decisions and have a more significant impact.

2. Financial Literacy: Develop a basic understanding of financial concepts such as revenue, profit, cash flow, and cost structure. Recognize the financial impact of HR decisions.

3. Stay Current: Stay curious about market trends, emerging technologies, and industry news. Engage with client groups, attend meetings, and explore external data points for a holistic understanding.

4. Network: Cultivate relationships for access to diverse ideas, perspectives, and potential partnerships. Networking opens doors to opportunities you might not have discovered otherwise.

Remember, business acumen involves not just knowledge but understanding, application, and continuous learning. Embrace curiosity and questioning, as it pays dividends in your career.

Drive your talent strategy with data

People analytics, a field that may evoke various emotions, is not new to HR, but its sophistication has evolved. While data scientists are integral to some HR teams, a general understanding of data is more crucial. Core components include:

1. Data Collection: Gather relevant data on areas like employee engagement, turnover, and productivity. The quality of data influences the value of insights.

2. Data Analysis: Use HR tech tools or platforms to analyze data, identifying patterns and insights that shape people programs.

3. Actionable Insights: Translate insights into actionable strategies. For instance, addressing high turnover by delving into the underlying issues.

4. Continual Monitoring: Data is an ongoing process. Monitor the impact of actions over time, adjusting strategies as needed.

Remember, data is a tool, and effective utilization can transform raw numbers into impactful business strategies.

Build trust and influence

Trust is pivotal for HR practitioners to make a meaningful impact. Here are seven key pillars for building trust:

1. Transparency: Counter stereotypes by openly explaining decisions. Transparent actions build trust in your judgment.

2. Consistency: Trust grows with time through reliable and consistent behavior. Align actions with words to avoid eroding trust.

3. Empathy: Demonstrate genuine interest, understanding, and compassion. Employees are more likely to stay if leaders show empathy.

4. Influence: Trust is the foundation of influence. Inspire others to follow your lead by establishing trust.

5. Expertise: Build trust by showcasing a strong knowledge base in HR and staying informed about industry trends and developments.

6. Communication: Effective communication, including active listening, enhances influence. Experiment with various communication platforms.

7. Networking: Forge strong relationships to expand your influence. Trust and influence are valuable assets for inspiring teams and advancing your career.

Navigate career ladders and lattices

HR's evolution has shifted from a linear career path to encompass diverse roles and talents. While traditional vertical ladders persist, career lattices, involving lateral moves, have gained prominence. The influx of professionals like marketers, engineers, data scientists, and project managers into HR, and vice versa, has transformed the field. This diverse experience challenges the singular perspective of HR, emphasizing both vertical and lateral growth. Vertical advancement provides depth, leadership skills, and increased responsibility. Lateral growth adds variety, business acumen, a broader skillset, and a growth mindset for adaptability. A balanced mix of both propels your career, offering depth and breadth, leadership, adaptability, specialization, and diversification. In today's dynamic business landscape, exploring various paths fosters continual learning and growth, presenting abundant opportunities for HR professionals.

Build your network equity

Your value to your employer is no longer solely determined by what you know; it's also about your network equity. In this era, cultivating a diverse and intentional network is crucial. Network equity leverages collective intellect from various experiences and perspectives, magnifying your impact. Building it requires generosity, adding value without expecting reciprocity. Actively create meaningful connections, diversify your network, and invest time in nurturing and maintaining relationships. Treat your network as an investment in your future, like a garden that, when nurtured, flourishes and bears fruit, enhancing your professional growth.

Honing your learning agility

As humans, we are constantly learning, whether intentionally or incidentally. Learning agility, crucial in the dynamic world of HR, involves seeking and applying new information, learning from experiences, and adapting to change. It empowers you to enhance project success by exploring new tools and methods. Curiosity, a key aspect of learning agility, fuels innovation by prompting questions, seeking knowledge, and challenging the status quo. In the ever-evolving field of HR, these skills are essential for thriving amidst change and chaos.

Chapter 2 AI and Workplace Transformation

Generative AI will bring exponential thinking

Understanding the significant impact of generative AI allows us to anticipate and prepare for the forthcoming changes. Rather than fearing AI replacing humans, the focus should be on humans utilizing AI to replace tasks performed without AI. Generative AI can create content in language, images, audio, video, and code, offering various applications such as generating text, coding, and automating tasks. McKinsey reports that a third of organizations regularly use generative AI, with notable productivity gains in tasks like customer inquiries and document generation. Embracing curiosity and adopting a learning mindset are essential for navigating the transformative impact of generative AI on the future of work.

The coming mega change transformation

Looking back to 1993 when the browser was invented, we couldn't have foreseen the current world. Similarly, looking ahead, generative AI will impact the workforce, with jobs created and lost. Goldman Sachs estimates up to half of all jobs may be affected, mainly in administrative and legal roles, with potential productivity gains within 18 months. In business strategy, generative AI creates growth opportunities, reminiscent of Barnes and Noble's dot-com era challenges. Customer experience will see improvements with AI handling routine queries, offering personalized responses, and enhancing interaction. While the upcoming changes may seem overwhelming, the key is to adapt to the evolving landscape.

Asking great questions to create alignment

In the early stages of AI transformation, leaders must shift from having all the answers to crafting great questions. Asking questions is challenging, especially when seen as challenging authority or the status quo. However, fostering a questioning and learning culture is crucial in the generative AI transformation. Encouraging questions from anyone in the organization, as everyone has access to generative AI, helps in this process. Essential questions to consider include focusing generative AI efforts, understanding changes in employee roles, ensuring transparency, and adapting leadership to support the workforce. Tips for asking great questions include being open-ended, exploratory, and seeking to learn or deepen understanding. Instead of asking if generative AI creates legal risk, inquire about the specific risks and ways to address them. Rather than questioning if generative AI will cause job loss, explore how jobs may change due to its influence.

Prioritizing your AI efforts

Generative AI is like a kid in a candy store — overwhelming with possibilities. To avoid use case paralysis, focus on the major buckets of automation, analytics, and optimization. Automation covers tasks like copywriting and customer service. Analytics democratizes data insights, empowering anyone with a good question. Optimization predicts and customizes products and services. To prioritize efforts, align generative AI with your current strategy and assess its impact. Identify preliminary use cases and rate them by strategic value and risk. This matrix helps prioritize initiatives based on their potential impact on strategic success.

How generative AI is changing roles and collaboration

Technology has historically created and eliminated jobs, and generative AI will follow suit. Initial job impacts will include automatable tasks like copywriting, social media management, call centers, and paralegals. Upskilling will be needed for roles reviewing AI-generated drafts, like software programmers assessing code. Reskilling will be necessary for roles that become obsolete, such as call center positions. Develop a roadmap for generative AI's impact on your workforce, considering upskilling, reskilling, and engaging internal leaders. Form an AI council reporting to a senior leader to align efforts with organizational strategy. This challenge and opportunity transcend HR and require collaboration across leadership roles.

Preparing your workforce for the changes to come

Understanding the truth is preferable to speculating about worst-case scenarios, so we aim to replace uncertainty with clarity. Transparency regarding job changes due to artificial intelligence is crucial. Keep your commitment to your employees central in all actions. Employees expect honesty and fairness; their perception depends on your readiness for this transformation. Anticipate and address their questions, concerns, fears, and anxieties. Be upfront about job shifts, creations, necessary training, and the timeline. Consider the role of managers in communication. Address their concerns early to enable confident communication. Define what managers convey and what leaders explain. Communicate proactively to instill confidence, involving executives and managers appropriately. Acknowledge uncertainties, outline plans (e.g., AI council), and commit to regular updates. Make leaders accessible for questions and ideas, providing a timeline for details. Establish channels for employees to share concerns, ideas, or questions, ensuring follow-up. Involve managers in sessions with leaders, always respond with honesty and fairness, even if the answer is uncertain. View this as an opportunity to strengthen relationships, understanding, and trust with employees.

Emerging skillsets of the AI era

Scaling generative AI in your organization demands a fresh skill set and mindset, influencing workforce changes through strategic training and hiring. Generative AI excels in personalized training, with a focus on upskilling the AI council, providing basic generative AI training for all, and enhancing general knowledge and skills across the board. Ensure responsible usage through a code of conduct and designate tools for specific job areas. Encourage generative AI as a co-pilot by creating prompt libraries and fostering collaboration. Leverage generative AI for training, emphasizing video creation tools. Prioritize individuals with a growth mindset for training and consider curiosity and adaptability when hiring and promoting. Acknowledge that not everyone may embrace upskilling, respecting individual choices. The diverse workforce requires a mix of new mindsets and skills.

Help your workforce thrive with AI

Leaders must anticipate and address the emotional needs of employees during transformative periods, creating a supportive environment. Beyond communication, responsible leaders foster psychological safety to help the workforce thrive with AI. Acknowledge the challenges of transformation, particularly the messy phase, where exploration and growth occur. Leaders provide stability by defining boundaries for experimentation, ensuring employees feel safe to step out of their comfort zones. Grant employees a sense of control in the transformation process, allowing them to have a say. Consider the impact of generative AI use cases on the workforce and identify significant changes employees will face. Embrace change, recognizing your role as a leader in guiding employees through it. Allocate time and space for the messy middle, offering support instead of rushing through the process.

Leading in the generative AI era

Similar to parenting teenagers, managing employees with generative AI involves acknowledging their newfound capabilities and desire for autonomy. Traditional command-and-control leadership models, like shepherding sheep, may not align with the increased agency generative AI provides. Shift leadership to a partnership model, focusing on defining objectives, boundaries, and guardrails instead of specific tasks. Embrace the shift by fostering good judgment and navigating the gray areas. Recognize that true control in relationships is elusive, and leadership involves growth and nurturing. Consider how generative AI can enhance employee autonomy and responsibility in specific use cases. Adapt your leadership style to encourage experimentation and empower employees to take initiative. Initially, establish guardrails for comfort, gradually allowing more freedom as confidence in their abilities grows. Embrace your transformation as a leader, recognizing the mutual benefits for you and your employees.

Key Generative AI Capabilities

1. Creative Content Generation:

  - Generates diverse content, including text, images, audio, video, and code.

2. Design and Innovation:

  - Sparks innovative ideas and concepts, facilitating efficient and creative design processes.

3. Personalization and Customization:

  - Tailors recommendations, products, or services to individual preferences, enhancing customer and employee satisfaction.

4. Discovery:

  - Generates and tests hypotheses, identifying patterns in data for breakthroughs in fields like medicine, chemistry, and material sciences.

5. Prediction, Automation, Efficiency:

  - Automates repetitive tasks in various domains such as data analysis, legal review, copywriting, customer service, and manufacturing.

6. Education:

  - Customizes learning materials for individual learners, creating interactive and engaging experiences to improve knowledge retention

Chapter 3 AI, Recruiting, and Talent Acquisition

Generative AI and the future of talent acquisition

Imagine if AI could write, converse, analyze data, and exhibit empathy as effectively as humans. Generative AI already possesses these capabilities, evolving daily. Talent acquisition professionals must contemplate its impact on roles, career paths, and the overall recruitment experience. Generative AI performs core recruitment tasks, necessitating professionals to identify where human input adds the most value. Applicants benefit from streamlined job searches, 24/7 conversational experiences, and personalized communications. Post-acceptance, generative AI aids onboarding and offers hyper-personalized career recommendations for employees. Hiring managers leverage self-service generative AI for automated sourcing, screening, interview scheduling, and data analysis. Its impact spans all facets of talent acquisition, necessitating a reevaluation of processes to optimize generative AI's potential. This transformative technology marks an exciting era for talent acquisition.

Identifying the various forms of generative AI

Explore the diverse landscape of generative AI beyond ChatGPT, with examples like Claude, Midjourney, VoiceBox, ElevenLabs, Synthesia, and HeyGen. Gen AI encompasses image, music, voice, and video generation, with new solutions emerging regularly. Large language models (LLMs) like ChatGPT excel in text generation and understanding, utilizing transformers in their neural networks. Numerous LLMs exist, including public models like Claude, LaMDA (powering Google's Bard AI), and Meta's LLaMA, along with custom models for HR tasks. Beyond text, Midjourney and Stable Diffusion produce stunning images from simple text prompts, eliminating the need for stock imagery. VoiceBox and ElevenLabs offer text-to-speech solutions with diverse voices, and some can even clone voices based on a person's input. Synthesia and HeyGen generate lifelike human avatars with voiceovers in numerous languages, facilitating easy video creation. Gen AI, beyond ChatGPT, is a versatile tool for enhancing talent acquisition processes, driving efficiencies, and improving overall experiences.

Visualizing how generative AI can be used in TA: Use cases

The most accessible use case for GenAI in recruitment is enhancing job descriptions and postings, but its capabilities extend beyond text generation. GenAI, such as Midjourney, can turn text into images, offering unique and personalized visuals for candidate outreach. Text-to-voice solutions humanize chatbots and allow personalized voice messages from hiring managers, even cloning voices for authenticity. Combining audio and video, GenAI enables quick video creation with lifelike avatars, supporting various languages and even cloning voices within the company. This versatile technology eliminates the need for expensive video shoots, allowing on-demand creation for testimonials, messages, and standardized candidate interviews. Consider inefficiencies in talent acquisition processes and explore how different forms of generative AI can enhance productivity and experiences.

How recruiters can use generative AI in talent acquisition

Generative AI offers positive impacts throughout the talent acquisition process. It can enhance job descriptions, postings, employer branding, and social recruiting content in various formats. GenAI aids sourcing by understanding natural language, allowing precise skill-based searches and conversational refinement. For outreach, it crafts customizable messages, incorporating images, audio, and video for engaging interactions. In pre-screening, GenAI-driven chatbots provide a human-level conversational experience, offering insights into company culture and applicant status. Evaluating applicants becomes more efficient with GenAI assisting in creating questions, scoring rubrics, and transcribing interviews. Post-acceptance, GenAI facilitates onboarding with tailored learning paths. It also supports brainstorming for talent acquisition and DEI strategies. Reflect on your talent acquisition process to identify where GenAI can have the greatest impact.

How generative AI can be used by candidates in recruiting

Job seekers using ChatGPT for resumes and cover letters raises ethical questions, but leveraging available tools is a common practice. Beyond application materials, Gen AI can enhance job search functionality on websites, ensuring more accurate and inclusive results. While using Gen AI for resumes aligns with professional resume writing services, caution is needed in screening questions and assessments. As ChatGPT has passed various exams, considered potential risks and explored changes to your processes. Detection tools for AI-generated text are unreliable, suggesting the use of proctored assessments. Job seekers can also utilize Gen AI to prepare for interviews by generating likely questions and ideal responses. Evaluate recruitment processes, minimize risks of unethical behavior, and prioritize fair and informed decision-making for a balanced talent acquisition experience.

How hiring managers can benefit from generative AI

What if hiring managers could complete recruiting tasks in just 15 minutes daily? With Gen AI and intelligent automation, this may become a reality. Gen AI simplifies talent acquisition for hiring managers, allowing them to create and post jobs, review applicants, schedule interviews, and negotiate offers effortlessly through a conversational interface. Personalized audio or video messages to top talent are achievable in minutes, enhancing candidate engagement. Gen AI supports proactive internal recruitment, analyzing talent supply, recommending candidates, and providing backfill suggestions. It aids in developing fair interview questions and scoring rubrics, ensuring consistent and unbiased evaluations. Leveraging Gen AI can significantly involve hiring managers in talent acquisition, promoting self-service capabilities and fostering fair and equitable outcomes. Reflect on how Gen AI could enhance hiring manager involvement in your company's talent acquisition process.

How generative AI can facilitate internal mobility

Can talent acquisition be applied to internal hires? Gen AI supports recruiters by enhancing internal mobility, reducing backfilling needs, and increasing retention. Traditional approaches like internal job boards often fall short, lacking efficiency and limiting employee access to relevant opportunities. Gen AI, with its natural language search and conceptual understanding, aids employees in finding suitable roles, accounting for adjacent skills. It proactively recommends jobs based on employee profiles, creating a low-friction, conversational experience for profile building. Gen AI helps employees explore career paths, conducts skill gap analyses, and proposes personalized learning plans. Continuous feedback ensures progress alignment with career goals. Gen AI offers numerous possibilities for internal mobility, improving employee experience, engagement, and retention while minimizing backfill recruiting pressures. Reflect on how Gen AI could enhance your company's internal mobility initiatives.

10 questions to ask vendors claiming to use generative AI

While GenAI in talent acquisition offers promising benefits, it comes with five crucial considerations. First, refrain from using GenAI for content intended for copyright claims. Second, exercise caution with public GenAI solutions, as they lack privacy guarantees for personal or confidential information. Third, acknowledge that GenAI can sometimes generate inaccurate information, particularly in critical tasks like compensation analysis. Fourth, biases in historical data can result in biased output, especially in language models trained on such data. Fifth, while GenAI can produce human-like text, it may lack creativity or deliver average output. It's essential to thoroughly review GenAI output for accuracy, bias, and quality before utilization.

When engaging with third-party or internal GenAI developers, pose key questions to ensure well-informed decisions. Consider asking the following:

1. Do you utilize our data to train your general model for others to benefit from the learnings?

2. How can your solution be customized for our company's specific needs?

3. How do you train your solution for our distinct use cases?

4. How do you control for hallucinations in the generated content?

5. What measures do you have in place to ensure the accuracy of the output?

6. How do you support the ability to explain the generated content?

7. How do you ensure that the output is fair and avoids biases, especially related to demographic factors?

8. What mechanisms are in place for the model to learn and adapt over time?

9. How do you ensure compliance with all applicable AI, automation, and data regulations?

10. Can you provide case studies or references from clients or users with similar requirements?

While embracing the opportunities presented by GenAI, it's crucial to remain mindful of its limitations and potential risks. Seek detailed answers from solution providers to ensure effective risk mitigation.

Where do humans fit in the future of AI-driven recruiting?

AI has the potential to automate a significant portion of the recruiting lifecycle, but automation isn't always advisable. Human involvement remains crucial in areas where empathy is essential. While AI, like ChatGPT, can mimic empathy effectively, forming genuine relationships in recruiting interactions is still a human domain. Recruiters play a vital role in understanding job seekers, building rapport, and influencing actions like responding to outreach, joining communities, and accepting offers.

Despite AI advancements, recruiters may shift towards becoming talent advisors, offering market intelligence and strategic guidance. Some may transition into career coaching roles, fostering relationships with applicants and supporting internal mobility and retention. Critical thinking and problem-solving, uniquely human skills, will remain valuable. While initial talent sourcing can be automated with Gen AI, recruiters specializing in high-demand profiles may stay relevant.

In a Gen AI-driven recruitment landscape, strategic decisions must be made about where to apply automation and where to maintain a human touch for a more people-centric experience. Fully automated experiences should be approached cautiously, considering people's strong negative feelings toward AI decision-making in the hiring process. Full compliance with regulations regarding automated decision-making is paramount.

Embracing generative AI as your recruiting copilot

To stay informed and capitalize on Generative AI benefits in recruitment while avoiding risks, follow these recommendations. Firstly, set up Google alerts for terms like ChatGPT and Generative AI, and combine them with recruiting, HR, o talent acquisition for daily content updates. Explore LinkedIn for AI and recruiting content and follow thought leaders in the field.

Secondly, embrace change and proactively reimagine the recruiting process with Gen AI. Identify areas for improvement and assess Gen AI's potential to drive enhancements. Thirdly, actively engage in your company's exploration of Gen A in talent acquisition. Participate in demos, evaluations, pilots, and proof of concepts. Safely experiment with free Gen AI solutions and contribute to corporate guidance on responsible Gen AI use.

Fourthly, prioritize the development of uniquely human skills such as empathy, relationship building, influence, creativity, critical thinking, and problem-solving. These skills enhance your effectiveness in talent acquisition. Treat Gen AI as a tool, understanding its capabilities to augment your abilities, drive efficiencies, and improve outcomes. Continually learn how to use evolving technologies like Gen AI while nurturing your uniquely human skills.

Chapter 4 AI in Learning and Development

Current challenges and opportunities in L&D

The demand for L&D leaders has been consistently rising post-pandemic and is expected to continue. As a leader, you play a crucial role in guiding organizations through evolving L&D strategies to foster a learning culture, stay relevant, and enhance employee retention. Challenges include aligning learning programs with business goals, addressing skill gaps through upskilling, securing budgetary support (which is generally positive), and managing time constraints. Leveraging GenAI presents an opportunity to overcome these challenges, align learning with business goals, and enhance productivity by 14%, enabling you to navigate the constant changes of the future of work effectively.

How generative AI can amplify and accelerate L&D outcomes

Gen AI offers a vast array of applications within L&D, including text, video, voice, and integrations. Examples include creating learning materials, personalized learning paths, and integrating learning into daily workflows. By using Gen AI, L&D leaders can demonstrate impact more effectively. For instance, they can design personalized learning paths for individuals, such as a customer service representative struggling with empathizing. This tailored approach incorporates simulations and assessments to enhance learning outcomes. In the next segment, we'll explore additional ways Gen AI can customize learning.

Designing customized learning programs

Research indicates that half of organizations develop in-house learning and development (L&D) programs, offering advantages in aligning with culture and priorities. However, L&D faces challenges in creating relevant materials due to resource constraints and the rapidly changing skills landscape. GenAI provides solutions: first, for topics and materials, it can analyze data to identify training topics and generate engaging, interactive learning materials. For example, if leaders struggle with managing remote teams, GenAI can create training focused on communication, inclusive leadership, and team building. Second, addressing the shelf-life issue, GenAI can evaluate program relevance and provide interactive brainstorming for updating content, aligning with business goals, and adapting to evolving needs, ensuring learning programs stay effective and aligned. Utilize GenAI to customize and extend the shelf life of your learning programs.

Generative AI and instructional design

In instructional design, two key challenges involve resource constraints for timely training aligned with business goals and adapting to dynamic learning trends like simulations and gamification. Gen AI enhances the ADDIE model, aiding in analysis by identifying learning needs and gaps. It generates objectives, outlines, storyboards, and learning activities in the design phase. In development, various Gen AI forms assist in creating materials, including simulations and gamification for engagement. For example, in sales training, it can generate customer role plays. In the implementation phase, Gen AI optimizes personalized learner experiences, while in the evaluation phase, it assesses course effectiveness. Gen AI serves as a valuable tool, complementing your instructional design expertise for unique and elevated learning experiences aligned with organizational goals.

Measuring effectiveness and data analysis

GenAI aids at all levels of the Kirkpatrick model—reaction, learning, behavior, and results. For instance, in a leadership development program, GenAI generates nuanced questions for reactions and analyzes responses for insights. It creates pre- and post-assessments, offering real-time feedback on learned skills. For behavior, it integrates with performance tracking systems and generates scenarios for evaluating leadership behaviors. Lastly, at the results level, GenAI analyzes data to demonstrate program effectiveness and ROI tied to key organizational metrics.

Upskilling and internal mobility

Managing upskilling and internal mobility is vital for competitive advantage, employer branding, recruitment, and retention. However, challenges arise due to time, resource constraints, and the need for effective learning. GenAI aids in mitigating these challenges by optimizing time, serving as research and planning tool, mapping current and future skills, and facilitating internal talent mobility. Whether for upskilling or internal mobility, GenAI supports strategy development, skill assessments, and identifying future skill needs for organizational adaptation.

Personalized, adaptive, and curated learning

L&D leaders grapple with the challenge of shifting from one-size-fits-all training to prioritizing learner-centric approaches for meaningful and relevant learning experiences. GenAI offers solutions through personalized, adaptive, and curated learning. Personalization tailors learning paths to employees' roles, strengths, weaknesses, aspirations, and development needs. For instance, a finance employee in the automotive industry struggling with forecasting can benefit from a personalized path with courses on financial modeling, economics, risk management, and industry specifics. This not only bridges skill gaps but also boosts motivation and engagement.

Adaptive learning, facilitated by GenAI, adjusts the pace and complexity based on real-time learner progress, ensuring effective and tailored learning experiences. Lastly, GenAI aids in curating up-to-date learning resources, from videos to podcasts, saving time and enriching day-to-day decisions. Leveraging

GenAI for personalized, adaptive, and curated learning fosters a culture of continuous learning and contributes to long-term organizational success. Reflect on how GenAI can enhance your people development strategies.

Developing business and use cases

To navigate the complex implementation, create a roadmap through use cases. Identify L&D challenges and select areas where GenAI can have a significant impact, such as content creation, learner engagement, upskilling, or personalized learning. Explore various GenAI tools (text, image, audio, video, code) suitable for addressing specific challenges. Consult key stakeholders, legal experts, and subject matter authorities to gather insights and brainstorm potential use cases. Prioritize use cases based on feasibility and organizational impact. Define measurable objectives and outcomes for each use case, aligning with your overall L&D strategy. Assess risks and devise mitigation strategies. Move to pilot testing, evaluate results, iterate as needed, and scale up. Continuously monitor, gather feedback, and adjust to ensure success. Given the evolving nature of GenAI, stay open to discovering new use cases and innovative applications. Developing use cases is an iterative and collaborative process, so embrace learning and adaptation along the way.

Legal and ethical considerations

Tech leaders, policy makers, and AI ethicists are actively shaping laws and guidelines for generative AI. As stewards of organizational culture, ensure ethical and legal implementation of GenAI. Key considerations include:

1. Copyright and Intellectual Property: Neglecting copyright and IP rights may lead to legal consequences. Verify the originality of GenAI-generated content to prevent copyright infringement and potential lawsuits. Regularly question and crosscheck content to avoid violations.

2. Data Privacy and Security: Noncompliance with data protection laws can result in fines and lawsuits. Ensure secure transmission of data to and from GenAI systems to prevent unauthorized access. Avoid exposing proprietary or confidential company information to protect competitive advantage.

3. Hallucinations and Bias: GenAI can produce incorrect content without ethical safeguards. Fact-checking is crucial to maintain trust and credibility. Avoid heavy reliance on GenAI as a primary information source and conduct audits for accuracy to safeguard learning quality.

4. Bias Mitigation: GenAI models trained on internet data may amplify bias. Develop a structured approach to identify and mitigate bias in personalized learning experiences. Address potential biases related to ethnicity, age, gender, and other factors to uphold equity and inclusion efforts.

Work collaboratively with your legal team to proactively minimize legal and ethical challenges associated with GenAI. Given its early stage, stay informed about evolving ethical and legal issues as you explore the potential of generative AI.

Visualizing the future of learning with generative AI

The future of L&D, intertwined with GenAI, is poised for growth, agility, and enhanced learning experiences. With numerous tools and integrations, it will be a competitive advantage for recruitment, engagement, and retention. This evolution allows for anticipatory, dynamic, and immersive learning experiences, even extending into the metaverse. Despite the rapid shift, L&D leaders can gain efficiency, effectiveness, and foresight from GenAI, fostering agility in aligning learning solutions with business goals. To lead effectively, enhance skills in human-centered design, storytelling, and consultative approaches. Improve knowledge in business strategy, data literacy, and AI fluency. As architects of the future, embrace the learning journey and shape your organization's path forward. Move forward together with confidence.

Chapter 5 Skills-First Recruiting

DEI recruiting: Order of operations

How do you view your current recruitment process? Regardless of your sentiments, there's always room for improvement, especially with the shift towards skills-based hiring. The traditional recruiting order involves sourcing, screening, interviewing, and hiring. Assessments, often overlooked or delayed, play a crucial role. Reflect on your current process—consider partnering with the learning and development team, review or create assessments, and assess skills earlier in the hiring process. If you can influence the process, propose updates. For those with limited influence, use this opportunity to enhance your skills in influence, strategy, and problem-solving.

Skills-based recruiting: Objectives and goals

For non-specialized jobs, demanding unnecessary degrees creates barriers to qualified candidates, disproportionately affecting minorities. A skills-based recruiting strategy is crucial for inclusivity. Despite companies emphasizing diversity, actions often fall short, contributing to a talent shortage. Eliminating biases and committing to true diversity recruiting is essential for success. A skills-first approach, as per LinkedIn, can boost talent pipelines significantly. Without recognizing the value in unconventional candidates, even a skills-based strategy can miss the mark.

Learning a new recruiting process

Are you advocating for a skills-first approach while lacking expertise in the strategy? Educate yourself on effective skills-based recruiting before expecting hiring managers to adopt it. Overcoming resistance is challenging, especially when leaders are reluctant to change established processes. Some fear that removing degree requirements lowers standards, but this mindset overlooks the diverse talents excluded by such criteria. Recognize the inequities, form a strategy, and promote a skills-first approach with a diversity, equity, and inclusion mindset.

A note about skills for recruiters

Recruiters, often immersed in LinkedIn, must possess essential skills such as communication, relationship building, adaptability, problem-solving, and business acumen. Operating in the middle ground between hiring managers and candidates can be challenging, requiring almost telepathic abilities. Adopting a skills-first approach aims to streamline and enhance the recruitment process, demanding recruiters to master essential skills while incorporating diversity, equity, and inclusion (DEI). Additional soft skills in DEI and hard skills in technology, particularly generative AI, are crucial for efficient and unbiased recruitment. Developing these skills ensures recruiters contribute effectively to the skills-first strategy, removing unnecessary barriers and fostering success.

Relationship building to meet hiring manager expectations

In recruiting, the common frustration arises when the hiring manager's expectations and the presented candidates don't align. To avoid this, enhance your influencing skills by reflecting on past effective instances and acknowledging the various underlying skills involved, including conflict resolution, communication, negotiation, teamwork, empathy, and patience.

Understanding that hiring managers seek interpersonal skills when they mention qualities like getting along well with others is crucial. Influencing and selling go hand in hand, making them vital recruiter skills. Strengthen your relationship with hiring managers by showcasing your ability to understand and assist them in achieving their goals. To succeed in skills-based recruiting, influence hiring managers to adopt the approach before rigid qualifications are set, emphasizing your role as the recruiter for the job.

Using critical thinking to identify competencies

Shifting the focus to competencies and skills instead of degrees broadens the recruitment pool, but it requires collaboration with hiring managers. Since they are not talent assessment experts, recruiters must guide and educate them on identifying essential skills. To facilitate this, ask questions about the role's day-to-day responsibilities, past expansions, and future expectations. This discussion helps distinguish hard and soft skills and clarifies necessary versus optional skills. When verifying skills, differentiate between aptitude tests and skills assessments. Tailor the assessment to the skill being evaluated, considering a DEI perspective. For example, in hiring an attorney, assess skills like relationship building and communication. Collaborating with hiring managers to create a skill-focused list ensures upfront agreement on assessment criteria. Ultimately, recruiters enhance critical thinking and patience, valuable skills in demand for recruiters.

Adjusting your sourcing strategy to consider equity

Identifying the skills needed streamlines the sourcing process in a skills-first approach, expanding the variety of candidate sources. Gaining upfront agreement on this strategy accelerates the recruitment process. For instance, IBM successfully filled critical skills gaps by tapping into diverse talent sources like coding camps, apprenticeship programs, and community colleges. To enhance diversity, recruiters should diversify their sourcing places, considering various educational institutions and events. In the intake process, discuss the sourcing strategy with hiring managers to secure agreement. Resistance to change is common but often stems from a reluctance to invest extra effort. Overcoming resistance involves demonstrating the benefits of the change, aligning it with the hiring manager's goals. For instance, showing how considering a broader range of candidates can lead to better outcomes. Data points can support this strategy, aiding in the conversation with hiring managers.

Aligning company value propositions with candidate values

As a recruiter, evaluating candidates is akin to completing a complex puzzle, requiring time and precision. Candidates seek companies valuing diversity and inclusive cultures, emphasizing authenticity and belonging. Utilizing listening and marketing skills, recruiters must understand candidate desires and sell the company, contingent on a robust employer value proposition. Conversations with hiring managers are crucial to uncover team values, problem-solving approaches, and developmental support for candidates. Recruiters face challenges when promoting companies as inclusive, especially when it may not align with reality. Tough questions involve ensuring inclusive language in job descriptions corresponds with the actual workplace environment. Recruiters must align personal values with their role to foster authenticity and inclusivity.

Demonstrating business acumen

For a successful skills-first approach in talent acquisition, alignment is crucial among recruiters, hiring managers, HR professionals, and others involved. While many companies predominantly follow a "buy" model, focusing on external talent, a holistic view involves incorporating the "build" model, emphasizing internal talent upskilling. In this approach, collaboration with learning and development (L&D) and talent management professionals is essential. Recognizing the importance of internal recruiting, 75% of professionals acknowledge its significance, with 81% emphasizing the need for close collaboration with L&D. Taking a proactive stance, a skills-first approach considers future business needs, allowing ample time for preparation.

Hershey's successful implementation involved building relationships with candidates well in advance, ensuring a ready pool for anticipated openings. Whether building or buying talent, strategic planning should consider the necessary runway, allowing time for relationship-building and awareness of market forces affecting future openings. Advising hiring managers requires attention to hiring trends, thorough intake meetings, and effective communication to ensure understanding of business needs. Recruiters must embrace a broader role, not just in acquisition but in influencing talent management processes and staying informed about current hiring trends and their business impact.

Your job is changing

Market demands, not the inherent nature of roles, often drive the requirement for degrees, serving as a means to narrow the candidate pool in an employer-driven market. However, recognizing when skills indicate job capability helps distinguish between a requirement and a barrier. Success lies in efficiently identifying and assessing skills crucial for business needs. Embracing a skills-first approach, which acknowledges that not every candidate needs a degree, expands the talent pool without compromising standards. Continuous upskilling is essential for recruiters to adapt to evolving job demands and identify candidates who can similarly adapt.

Chapter 6 Engaging and Retaining Gen Z with a Skills Approach

Embracing a human-centric approach

The evolution of technology has transformed consumer and business behaviors, particularly accelerated by the pandemic. Adapting to digitalized business operations is crucial, with customers expressing their feedback on social media. Businesses must respond swiftly to stay competitive, as seen in Zoom's introduction of 400 features in 2020. The shift to non-routine jobs has led to the emergence of the project economy, requiring collaboration in multi-generational teams. Managers play a vital role in engaging employees, especially younger cohorts, amid complex challenges. With a focus on a human-centric approach, businesses must elevate talent across all levels to thrive in the technology-driven era.

Recognizing Generation Z realities

In 2022, complaints about Generation Z being entitled to work from home echo previous sentiments about millennials seeking purpose and work-life balance in 2016. The recurring themes reflect leaders' reactions to changing work realities. Gen Z acknowledges the need for lifelong learning, prompting early promotions. Automation accelerates the advancement of entry-level tasks, exposing new hires to more advanced roles. Job security concerns lead to requests for flexible work arrangements. Enterprises flatten, requiring Gen Z to navigate non-linear careers and contribute actively in less hierarchical relationships. Strategies like contractor arrangements and side hustles reflect efforts to reduce risk and ensure financial stability. To bridge generational gaps, a reevaluation of interpretations and responses based on new realities is essential.

Shifting to skills in the new era of work

New job roles are constantly emerging, ranging from generative AI detectors to metaverse designers. To prepare for an unpredictable future, essential skills include problem-solving, adaptability, collaboration, and basic technical proficiency. The World Economic Forum identifies AI, machine learning, cloud computing, project management, and social media as the fastest-growing skills in 2023. Traditional job titles and degrees are becoming less relevant, with companies like MassMutual eliminating titles to focus on individual contributions. As technology evolves, the youngest employees may experience role reassignments. Developing core transferable skills, such as coding, data analysis, communication, and leadership, is crucial for navigating changing tasks and roles. Employers should identify and nurture skills aligned with business needs, providing opportunities for employees to acquire new skills through various means. Emphasizing "power skills," including empathy, communication, and negotiation, is vital for effective collaboration and managing diverse projects. Adopting a skills-first approach enables proactive upskilling for current and future needs.

Orienting toward a skills economy

Identifying your top three skills can be challenging for many, but it's crucial, especially for self-employed individuals whose success relies on showcasing their capabilities. In the evolving landscape of remote work and changing job requirements, adopting a skills-first approach is vital. To implement this approach, leaders should create a skills inventory and taxonomy, compiling current skills, education, and experiences, and classifying them into groups. Employee skills cards, inspired by Ray Dalio's concept, serve as dynamic, self-identifying documents to facilitate collaboration. Managers can align employees' roles with their skills, enhancing engagement and boosting revenues. Companies are shifting towards skill-focused hiring, minimizing the importance of traditional job titles. Gusto, for example, transitioned to functional descriptions in 2016, emphasizing contributions over titles. This skills-centric approach extends to career development and recruiting, emphasizing skills in external communications to attract talent, particularly appreciated by Gen Z.

Applying skills to optimize outcomes

Analyze the situation and recognize the skills we use to achieve results. Rally the team to finish the project and talk him through things; he looks overwhelmed. Embrace a skills-first approach to understand the specific skills applied in tasks and problem-solving, enhancing and acquiring skills for more effective collaboration. For instance, Antonio, the new sales manager, acquired video editing and empathy skills for better communication. Emphasize team and task-related skills, making it pervasive in career development for Gen Z employees. Map progression steps, check off acquired skills, and plan to acquire the rest. Accelerate adoption by reviewing and rewarding skill practices. Recognize effective communication or campaign success.

Empathizing with Gen Z's perspectives

Samantha and Ryan, leading Gen Z project teams, faced contrasting situations. Samantha criticized a team member without understanding the context, affecting team morale. Ryan, emphasizing proactivity, empathy, and curiosity, handled a similar scenario differently. He reached out to Taylor, a remote worker, proactively, demonstrating empathy by understanding his perspective, and approached the situation with curiosity, avoiding assumptions. Ryan's open-ended questions and active listening created a supportive environment, fostering engagement and successful collaboration with Gen Z team members.

Identifying trust disparities

Henry, a 25-year-old employee, faces disheartenment due to monitoring software inaccuracies and his Gen X boss's lack of trust and understanding in digital marketing technologies. This scenario is not unique, as widespread employee monitoring is observed in over half of surveyed large corporations, with 80% expected to adopt similar technologies by 2020. Trust, a crucial factor in employee engagement and innovation, is hindered by surveillance measures. Additionally, a Pew research study reveals that 60% of young adults lack trust, attributing it to concerns about societal issues, including climate change, job readiness, education costs, and retirement uncertainties. Leaders can address this challenge by fostering open communication, encouraging discussions about employees' personal and professional concerns, and practicing empathy to bridge generational gaps and build enduring trust with Gen Z employees.

Respecting Generation Z's goals

Consider your initial work goals and the available professional options. Contrast this with the current landscape for Gen Z, facing an array of choices, including more accessible entrepreneurial pathways. Empathy reveals that Gen Z's goals may be near-term due to evolving business landscapes, lack of job security, and a focus on transferable skills. Understand that their aspirations often center on immediate relevance and ongoing skill development. Encourage them to identify motivating objectives without fixating on predefined career paths, fostering adaptability and engagement. Recognize personal and evolving ambitions, guide them periodically, and help set realistic targets with reasonable timeframes for short and long-term professional growth.

Connecting with Gen Z's concerns

Understand the evolving priorities of Gen Z by engaging your empathy skills. Recognize their unique perspectives influenced by cultural shifts, emphasizing the desire for meaningful work and positive impact on the world. Acknowledge their concerns about financial stability, influenced by past economic events. When discussing learning objectives, consider their determination to maintain a competitive edge. Be attentive to mental health discussions, as depression and anxiety are prevalent among Gen Z. Address their worries to enhance engagement and performance in the fluid and uncertain technology-driven work landscape, fostering motivation, management, and longer-term retention.

Acknowledging Gen Z's needs

As a manager, invest time in getting to know each Gen Z team member, understanding their strengths, preferences, and work habits. Use empathy skills to tune into their unique points of view, learning styles, and reactions under pressure. Show support for their future growth early on and foster trust-based relationships through regular interactions, both virtual and in-person. Tailor guidance, processes, and boundaries to accommodate each individual's needs, optimizing their contributions. Be attentive to signals that indicate when to step in and offer support. Acknowledge the role of side hustles for financial stability and autonomy, recognizing their diverse interpretations of work. Understanding your team members' drives and energy sources helps you foster long-term engagement and excellence, both individually and as a team.

Nurturing cultural community

Establishing a strong company culture is crucial for success, shaped by the organization's mission and vision. For instance, Apple's emphasis on creative innovation reflects a culture that values challenging norms. Cultures are built on enduring values that guide employee behavior both in and out of the office. Communication skills play a key role in articulating timeless values like trust, empathy, open-mindedness, and inclusion. Reinforce these values consistently, emphasizing their meaning to all stakeholders, from employees to partners. Trust in Gen Z employees can be nurtured through activities like seeking their help, confirming understanding, facilitating open debates, fostering a sense of safety and belonging, and increasing transparency. These efforts contribute to a lasting community spirit and reinforce trust as a fundamental cultural value.

Fostering a flexible environment

Do you have specific tasks you find more productive to do from home? Many employees, including US Gen Zs, express a desire for flexible working hours and remote options. Recognizing the evolving needs of customers and the agility required in a dynamic market, leaders should embrace flexibility as a business imperative. Providing reasonable autonomy over work location, schedule, and tasks is crucial, especially for Generation Z. Workplace flexibility, as advocated by management guru Peter Drucker, is not just a policy but a mindset emphasizing inclusiveness. Use empathy to customize options for individual preferences, prioritize team preferences, and ensure leadership motivates flexible practices. Adopting a remote-first mindset, create routines that enhance the inclusion of remote workers and adapt to evolving team configurations. Your empathetic and adaptable leadership will help Gen Z employees navigate flexible work arrangements effectively.

Attracting Generation Z

In 2022, Redpoint Ventures, a prominent U.S. venture capital firm, utilized TikTok to engage with Gen Z. They posted brief, engaging videos featuring young entrepreneurs and experienced venture partners, aiming to connect with potential investees and future hires. Recognizing the importance of meeting Gen Z where they are, the company employed a millennial with digital expertise to enhance their brand communication. Similarly, in recruiting, it's crucial to build trust from the start. Provide honest, consistent messaging aligned with corporate values, offering authentic insights into the company culture and work environment. Focus on skills rather than schools or previous titles when discussing job fit with Gen Z candidates. Emphasize growth opportunities and align their potential career trajectories with the company's growth, showing a commitment to their future.

Leading through change

General Motors, a company with over 150,000 employees worldwide, emphasizes trust and transparency in its mission statement. In May 2021, CEO Mary Barra reiterated this trust by introducing a flexible work policy with the directive "work appropriately," conveying trust in employees to make responsible decisions during changing times. As a corporate leader, it's essential to demonstrate trust and uphold company values through actions and words, fostering a culture of responsibility and coaching over command. This shift involves yielding control, empowering Gen Z employees with more responsibility and data for informed decision-making. To transition effectively, facilitate collaborative meetings, show vulnerability as a leader, and embrace failure as a part of the learning process. Inform and empower your teams to contribute and execute effective strategies during times of uncertainty.

Designing the "how" of work

Generative AI, particularly ChatGPT, sparked concerns in late 2022 about potential job disruptions in various fields. Jobs like computer programming, data analysis, technical writing, advertising content creation, paralegal work, and market research were highlighted. As AI continues to evolve, particularly in automating entry-level tasks, it's crucial to use critical thinking skills to assess how organizational operations and roles are changing. This involves adapting processes, such as market exploration, and considering the impact on younger employees who work across locations and time zones. Collaborate with IT to analyze upgraded systems, design flexible process alternatives, and test updated workflows. Modernize documentation protocols to support decentralized decision-making and enhance asynchronous communication. Provide guiding building blocks and routines to give Gen Z autonomy and foster effective collaboration.

Supporting employee well-being

Research in 2022 revealed higher mental health struggles among US and UK Gen Zs compared to other generations. To attract and retain Gen Z employees, companies should offer holistic well-being programs covering physical health, mental health, stress management, financial resources, sustainability projects, and career growth opportunities. Normalize discussions about mental health to destigmatize it, and establish well-being practices, such as defined working hours, regular breaks, and community activities, to support Gen Z's overall well-being. Pay attention to subtle signals during check-ins and recommend confidential resources when needed. Knowing your Gen Z employees well helps in fostering good mental health and building a supportive corporate community.

Developing Gen Z talent

Boomer entrepreneur Damien, building an online adventure travel portal, hires Gen Z interns to gain job experience. He encourages them to explore travel categories, prompting internal and external research, skill experimentation, and discussions about future possibilities. Recognize their achievements, encourage targeted growth, provide regular feedback, and help them discover strengths and interests. Organize mentorships, coffee chats with managers, and self-reflection. Guide them in crafting career trajectories, planning upskilling, and facilitating transitional experiences. Cultivate relationships with leaders across departments to offer mobility and diverse learning opportunities. Proactively engage and support Gen Z employees to enhance retention.

Chapter 7 Increasing Learning Engagement

Why skills-first training?

Skills-based training emphasizes not just knowing but doing. While knowledge is essential for skill performance, mastery requires the practical application of that knowledge to achieve results, whether in coaching or troubleshooting high-tech equipment. Practice is crucial for skill development, yet the emphasis on practice tends to diminish with age. Engaging and interactive skills training should include dedicated time for employees to practice, extend to skill transfer across different contexts, and involve reflective sessions for learners to strategize optimal skill utilization. Skills training, with a focus on application, practice, and generalization, cultivates high-performing, adaptable individuals, setting the stage for long-term success in both individuals and organizations.

What are power skills?

Power skills, formerly known as soft skills, are essential for individual success, encompassing abilities like interpersonal communication, social and emotional intelligence, critical thinking, coaching, teamwork, leadership, professional attitude, work ethic, problem solving, and listening. The term "soft skills" initially downplayed their significance, implying they were easy to learn and master. However, these interpersonal skills play a crucial role in effective teamwork, decision-making, communication, and organizational leadership. Recognizing their value, organizations now emphasize power skills development, leading to increased profitability, cooperation, and overall success. In a globally connected world, power skills are vital for staying competitive in the workplace. Choosing not to invest in power skills training puts individuals and organizations at a disadvantage, while those who prioritize it gain a significant edge.

What are hard skills?

Hard skills are either known or not, representing specific, measurable, and industry-specific technical abilities required for particular jobs. These skills, such as programming for a software engineer or chemical manufacturing processes for a chemical engineer, are often transferrable across industries. They follow exact rules, directions, or instructions, with standard operating procedures ensuring consistency. While some hard skills involve step-by-step procedures, others allow variations in the application. Many jobs require employees to combine various hard skills, like a customer service representative using ordering software, querying databases, and utilizing spreadsheets based on customer requests. Identifying the necessary hard skills for each role is crucial for creating engaging and interactive instructional content.

Identifying response attributes

Power skills hinge on responding effectively with the right tone, approach, and content. Traditional training often falls short by presenting pre-written responses for learners to choose without exploring the reasoning behind them. To address this, encourage learners to identify attributes of a response that make it appropriate for a given situation. For example, in customer service training, instead of providing answer choices, present a list of attributes related to tone, approach, and content. This approach, called "identifying response attributes," fosters higher-order thinking, allowing learners to generalize power skills to various situations. Consider implementing this training technique to enhance your team's response capabilities.

In medias res

The term "in medias res," Latin for "in the midst of things," is commonly used in entertainment to plunge the audience into the action without prior setup. This technique, when applied to soft skills training, creates engaging instruction. In a physical, virtual, or e-learning setting, start without stating instructional objectives. Instead, present a dilemma or question for immediate learner engagement. For instance, in a fraud investigation class, I began with a scenario of a coworker suspecting the boss of embezzlement. Learners responded, and through a mock investigation, they explored the topic actively. This approach captivates learners, fostering a more impactful learning experience. Create your own in medias res training by crafting scenarios, identifying a critical point, posing a question, and using learner responses to teach soft skills effectively, whether in negotiation or leadership. This technique, whether live, virtual, or in e-learning, immediately involves learners, creating a compelling and teachable moment.

Construct activity

Most power skills are grounded in specific models like sales, negotiation, or leadership models, each with defined steps for achieving desired outcomes. Construct activities, based on constructivism, involve learners in building their understanding of a skill. To create such an exercise, choose a model for the power skill, present its elements without a visual, and have learners, in groups or individually, arrange these elements into their own model. Encourage the use of shapes, images, and arrows to enhance comprehension. After creation, learners explain their models to the class, allowing for discussion on similarities and divergences from the official model. Incorporating freeform response in self-paced e-learning modules also aids learners in constructing their understanding of power skills.

Role-play with a twist

Role-playing is a valuable method for practicing power skills like negotiation and sales, but it can be met with reluctance from learners. To address this, engage all learners in the process by creating an observational checklist for those not directly involved in the role play. In self-paced eLearning, transform role plays into branching scenarios, allowing learners to make decisions with consequences. Alternatively, convert role-playing exercises into card games, whether physical or online, where learners respond to scenarios and receive feedback from peers. These strategies enhance engagement and effectiveness while making the learning experience enjoyable.

Card and board games for skills reinforcement

Card and board games have emerged as a surprising and effective method for teaching soft skills, offering repetitive practice without the monotony of repeated exercises. These games can be particularly engaging, fostering skill development through enjoyable repetition. For instance, a board game was created to enhance critical thinking among business unit leaders, guiding them to consider enterprise-wide issues. The game, played in rounds, facilitated coaching on optimal problem-solving approaches. Traditional games, when digitized, like the Enterprise Game Stack for sorting games, add multimedia elements, enhancing the learning experience. Leveraging the simplicity and widespread understanding of these games, incorporating them into soft skills training proves to be a valuable strategy.

Learning by doing: A three-step process

An effective method for teaching hard skills, whether in a classroom or an e-learning module, is the three-step learning-by-doing process known as "show me, guide me, let me try." Initially, learners receive a demonstration of the skill, followed by a guided practice with instructions and feedback. Finally, learners have the opportunity to independently apply the skill. For instance, a training course on avionics equipment uses this process, allowing learners to progress from a demonstration mode to a guided practice mode and ultimately to practicing on their own. This interactive approach builds necessary skills while providing support and guidance when needed.

Whiteboard walk-through

Skills-based training aims to equip individuals with the ability to perform technical procedures, such as programming machinery or troubleshooting code, by following a step-by-step process. One effective method for reinforcing this training is through a whiteboard exercise, which can be conducted on a virtual or physical whiteboard, flip chart, or paper. Instruct learners on the procedure and relevant information, then have them pair up to draw and explain the process to each other. This exercise exposes gaps and misunderstandings in their knowledge, prompting them to address and enhance their understanding of the skill. The whiteboard exercise can also be adapted for self-paced e-learning with a drag-and-drop activity to sequence steps and answer related questions, providing a valuable tool for self-assessment and learning reinforcement.

Applied practice

To become proficient in hard skills like coding or manufacturing, learners benefit from dedicated practice time in an environment that mirrors real-world conditions. While exact physical replicas, as seen in the nuclear power plant example, are not always feasible, online versions or replicas offer opportunities for learners to practice and enhance their skills. These environments, whether immersive 360-degree videos or simulated games, can't replace on-the-job training but can accelerate the learning process, shorten training time, and provide valuable additional feedback not readily available in the actual setting. Consider creating applied practice environments, such as online simulations or games, to prepare employees before engaging in on-the-job training.

Observational checklist as a learning tool

An observational checklist is more than an evaluation tool; it serves as a valuable aid for learners to understand, practice, and apply hard skills effectively. Initially, provide learners with the checklist to outline the sequential steps required for the skill. During a video or live demonstration, have learners check off items, ensuring they recognize subtle aspects of the skill. Additionally, employ the checklist for self-assessment, enabling learners to rate their performance and identify areas for improvement. Encourage learners to create their checklist and compare it with an expert's, fostering a deeper understanding of skill application. Integrating observational checklists into instruction enhances learning and self-evaluation, contributing to skill proficiency.

Escape room design

When developing hard or technical skills, integrating troubleshooting and problem-solving practices is crucial. A compelling approach is to implement an escape room-style activity, where learners solve puzzles or challenges to achieve a specific goal. Whether in a physical or virtual setting, this design offers context and urgency, simulating real-world scenarios. Define the troubleshooting skills, establish a desired outcome, and craft challenges aligned with the skills. Form groups, present the escape room, and immerse learners in a meaningful and time-sensitive learning experience. Utilizing an escape room design enhances engagement and skill application in troubleshooting training.

Chapter 8 Creating Inclusive Learning Experiences

The foundations of an inclusive learning experience

Inclusive learning embraces the principle of adapting teaching methods to suit diverse learning styles and preferences. It thrives in an open environment where every learner feels heard, seen, and empowered to pursue ambitious learning goals. To foster inclusivity, follow the three foundational principles—the three B's. The first B is to "be aware" of personal biases and their potential impact on learning experiences. Identifying and mitigating biases ensures a balanced approach. The second B is to "bring authenticity" to learning experiences. Being genuine creates a stronger connection with learners, allowing them to feel more comfortable being themselves. The final B encourages the need to "build bonds and bridges" before learning begins. Establish connections through humor or inspiration to engage learners on a human level, fostering a positive and inclusive learning environment.

Why creating inclusive learning experiences matters

Inclusive learning experiences matter for three key reasons. Firstly, they provide the opportunity for each individual to learn in their unique way, catering to diverse learning styles through carefully crafted modules. Secondly, inclusive learning minimizes the distinctness of differences, fostering a space where diverse strengths and challenges coexist. Encouraging learner interaction facilitates common ground discovery and promotes collaboration. Lastly, inclusive learning instills a sense of anticipation and excitement, drawing learners from various backgrounds and perspectives. By creating experiences that cater to all, organizations elevate their learning programs, inspiring learners to reach their full potential.

The INCLUDE model

To create inclusive learning experiences, use the INCLUDE model, focusing on seven key areas. Begin by investigating the needs of your learners, followed by identifying elements that nourish their unique hunger for learning. Collaborate with stakeholders to build a well-rounded learning experience. Prioritize listening to ensure learner-centricity and then unite learners through participation, fostering compassion. Provide a discovery environment for self-paced learning. Finally, empower learners by recognizing your role in shaping the learning environment. Address each step before progressing to build truly inclusive experiences.

Investigate the needs of your learners

Investigation is the crucial first step in the INCLUDE model, which I use to enhance learning experiences. Investigating involves thorough research to understand the genuine reasons behind learners' training needs. Employ the four P questions: Identify patterns impacting performance, address current problems hindering business objectives, align learning initiatives with strategic priorities, and explore pain points for HR teams. This intentional investigation ensures a laser-focused approach to creating impactful learning experiences that drive organizational impact.

Identify design elements that nourish

The "Nourish" step in the INCLUDE model focuses on providing elements that satisfy learners' hunger for impactful learning. To achieve this, explore diverse design elements such as the 1-2-4-All method for inclusive participation, a gallery walks to engage learners in exploring content, and the circle-square-triangle method for reflection. Additionally, utilize resources like learning battlecards, offering a variety of learning design methods. By incorporating these methods, you not only nourish your learners but also enhance inclusivity and engagement in your learning experiences.

Collaborate with multiple stakeholders to develop the learning experience

In the early stages of my career, I was eager to provide value through impactful learning experiences. However, I realized the importance of collaborating with key stakeholders who could contribute valuable insights and help navigate potential challenges. Creating inclusive learning experiences, as outlined in the INCLUDE model (Investigate, Nourish, Collaborate, Listen, Unite, Discover, and Empower), is akin to being a skilled race car driver who relies on a proficient pit crew. The collaboration step involves forming a "learning crew" comprising three essential stakeholders: the learner, HR partner, and diversity, equity, and inclusion (DE&I) expert. Engaging these individuals early and consistently ensures the learning experience resonates with diverse needs, aligns with broader HR strategies, and incorporates an inclusion lens. Reflect on your upcoming learning experience and identify your learning crew to drive success and inclusivity.

Listen to your learners

In the INCLUDE model (Investigate, Nourish, Collaborate, Listen, Unite, Discover, and Empower), the fourth step, "Listen," is pivotal. Shifting from instructor-centered to learner-centered listening involves questioning preconceptions, adopting a curious mindset, and focusing on learners' needs. Connect with learners by moving from talking at them to connecting during various interactions. Establish feedback loops to enhance communication and promote a learner-centric environment. Evaluate recent learning experiences and take incremental steps for a more inclusive and learner-centric approach.

Foster participation that unites

Deloitte's research reveals that over 61% of surveyed employees cover part of their identity at work, impacting engagement and productivity. In the INCLUDE model (Investigate, Nourish, Collaborate, Listen, Unite, Discover, and Empower), the fifth step is "Unite," crucial for creating a learning environment that encourages full participation without covering aspects of one's identity. To foster participation that unites, focus on creating a brave space that encourages dialogue, contribution, and recognizes each learner's unique value. Questions to consider include: Have I created a space for compassion? Encourage participants to share vulnerability through "I am" statements. Are participants confident in their ability to learn? Assess engagement in the initial workshop minutes. Am I sparking curiosity about learners' strengths? Foster meaningful interactions across diverse backgrounds to deepen engagement and connections. Learning experiences can unite people, fostering a deeper understanding of themselves, creating connections, and impacting engagement and performance.

Promote an environment where people can discover

Often, we witness new managers disengaged during training sessions on delegation and micromanagement, hindering their effectiveness. The INCLUDE model's sixth step, "Discover," emphasizes creating an environment for personalized learning. Utilizing discovery learning, learners find information independently, fostering engagement and affirming their unique learning styles. Practical approaches include one-to-one interviews, allowing learners to explore challenges and cultural influences independently. The cafeteria learning method offers an exploratory experience with diverse learning choices, accommodating various preferences. Discovery maps, constructed visuals, facilitate meaningful dialogue during significant organizational changes. Instead of instructing, encourage learners to pull information from their backgrounds, enhancing inclusivity in the learning environment.

Empower your learners

Research indicates that disempowerment leads to frustration, demoralization, reduced productivity, and disengagement. In workshops, learner empowerment is crucial for success. The seventh step of the INCLUDE model, "Empower," focuses on the facilitator's responsibility to instill confidence in learners. Inclusive prework ensures engagement, catering to diverse learning modalities. Quick coaching during workshops involves personalized discussions, linking concepts to real-world scenarios. Providing takeaway tools, such as reference guides or additional videos, empowers learners to apply newfound knowledge. Prioritizing empowerment cultivates lifelong learners, resilience, and stronger leadership, fulfilling the responsibility to stretch and empower learners.

Debunking myths about inclusive learning experiences

I recall a college experience where cramming for a test proved to be a failed strategy, debunking the myth that it works. Similarly, there are myths about creating inclusive learning experiences that need addressing. The first myth is that inclusivity happens naturally; in reality, it demands attention and intentionality. Another myth is that inclusive learning is merely a nice-to-have, while it is increasingly critical for diverse learners. The common myth that one must be an inclusion expert is challenged by the abundant resources available, such as courses on platforms like Catalyst.org. Don't let myths hinder your ability to deliver the inclusive learning experiences crucial for your organization's success.

Top tips for creating inclusive learning experiences

Consider what you're learning experiences are known for and what you want them to be known for as you apply the resources and approaches. To consistently create inclusive learning experiences, establish ground rules for success, model inclusive language, integrate inclusion into learning strategies, and foster an inclusive climate. Ground rules set the tone for an inclusive environment, inclusive language ensures engagement regardless of backgrounds, building inclusion into strategies creates safe spaces, and fostering a climate involves introducing preferred pronouns and showcasing diversity in examples and stories. These tips, along with your current efforts, can optimize contributions and remove barriers to inclusive learning experiences.

Chapter 9 Advancing a Diversity Strategy in Your Organization

Defining diversity, equity, inclusion, and belonging

Diversity encompasses the mix of employee backgrounds, identities, and experiences. Inclusion involves actively ensuring each individual feels welcomed and involved in conversations and decisions, while belonging is the profound feeling of being valued for one's unique qualities. Equity is foundational to all these concepts, focusing on achieving equal outcomes for different groups and recognizing the need for varied tools.

Implementing DEI as a strategic business effort

Recognizing that diversity, inclusion, and belonging (DIBs) require year-round commitment, it's crucial to move beyond viewing DIBs as occasional programs. To truly integrate DIBs into your organization, make it part of everyday business goals. Start with fostering a sense of belonging for diverse talent. While challenging, creating an inclusive environment benefit both employees and customers. Regardless of your role, contribute to making DIBs a strategic effort. Senior leaders can connect team efforts to the DIBs strategy, model inclusive behaviors, and champion diverse hiring. People managers should engage team members, ensuring everyone has a voice, while individual contributors can consider diverse customer needs and understand teammates' individual requirements. You don't need a diversity title to drive change in your organization.

Evaluating your organization's readiness

Consider your company's growth phase, avoiding the glass cliff phenomenon, especially during crises. Evaluate your organizational systems, deciding whether to create new ones or modify existing ones to embed DIBs. Examine your company culture, distinguishing between transactional and relational approaches. Prioritize authenticity and invest in trust-based relationships to create a safe environment for underrepresented groups and align with DIBs goals.

Designing with DEI in mind is everyone's job

A common misconception is that diversity, inclusion, and belonging (DIBs) are solely the responsibility of the talent-focused team. However, achieving DIBs goals involves collaboration and shared buy-in across all functions and levels. For successful diversity recruitment, collaboration with hiring managers and referrals is crucial. Building trusting relationships with diverse professionals is essential for a more inclusive talent pipeline. In organizations with high belonging, turnover is lower, and health outcomes are higher. Intentional inclusion in every interaction is necessary, and reflection helps foster inclusivity Reflect on questions like inviting diverse opinions and prioritizing concerns. Everyone plays a role in keeping customer diversity in mind, whether in product design or event planning. Talent-focused and customer-focused DIBs goals require intentional actions from everyone. Make it a habit to consider DIBs in your daily tasks.

Building equity into talent systems and processes

When discussing diversity, inclusion, and belonging, visible programs are often mentioned, such as resource groups or networking events. However, the less visible aspects, like talent processes, play a crucial role in determining access to opportunities. The talent life cycle, an unseen system, requires embedding equity for positive outcomes. Applying an equity lens across recruitment, performance evaluation, talent development, career advancement, and separation involves using the three S's: Structure (a defined process), Standards (clear criteria), and Sponsor (expectation for consistency). Building equity in talent systems enhances employee trust and perceptions of fairness in key talent decisions.

Applying the three S framework

The three S's talent lifecycle focusing on performance evaluation and career advancement. For performance evaluation, establish clear processes (Structure), define criteria in advance (Standards), and address disparities across identity groups (Sponsor). In terms of career advancement, implement standard promotion processes (Structure), define promotion criteria with shared understanding (Standards), and ensure consistent application of criteria (Sponsor).

Building equity into your product

If you're involved in product or service design, ensure it serves every user, dedicating resources to address diverse needs. Globally, 15% of the population experiences some form of disability, emphasizing the importance of inclusive design. Extend these considerations to various roles, such as sales, where understanding diverse client needs and building interpersonal skills is crucial. Make a habit of considering the "canary in the coal mine" – include vulnerable audiences or unlikely scenarios in your product design process.

Practicing a learner mindset

Many hesitate to act on diversity, inclusion, and belonging intentions due to fear and perceived risks, like making mistakes or being judged. Embracing a learner mindset in your company culture is essential for embedding DIBs, where mistakes are viewed as opportunities for growth and learning. Achieving this requires humility, acknowledging mistakes, and staying curious within healthy boundaries. Accountability is crucial for a DIBs learner mindset, involving repairing harm by apologizing and committing to change, and setting aspirational goals for future success.

Setting a tone of inclusion and belonging in leadership

Senior leaders play a crucial role in shaping an organization's diversity, inclusion, and belonging goals. They should commit to a personal journey of deepening awareness and emotional intelligence, embracing mistakes as part of the learning process. Senior leaders must actively sponsor individuals from underrepresented backgrounds, drive intentional career growth, and foster inclusive team norms. Investing in inclusive hiring practices, emphasizing diversity in referrals, and promoting a "culture add" approach are vital steps. By demonstrating the importance of DIBs through actions, senior leaders set the tone for the entire organization.

Fostering belonging as a people manager

Exceptional people managers recognize that diversity, inclusion, and belonging are integral to their role. They embrace an inclusive leadership skill set, acknowledging the importance of vulnerability and understanding individual differences. Self-awareness is a crucial aspect, allowing managers to identify and address biases. They actively listen to diverse perspectives, fostering a sense of belonging within their teams. Exceptional managers create a safe space for authenticity, encourage clear feedback, and remain mindful of team concerns, especially during challenging events. The key focus is on continuous personal growth and understanding how one's experiences shape their management approach, promoting inclusivity and deepening belonging.

Activating allyship

Allyship, as I define it, is an ongoing process of unlearning, reevaluating, and actively supporting others. It involves building relationships based on trust, consistency, and accountability rather than being an identity. Allies, typically those with historical power, learn about the experiences of underrepresented individuals and work to disrupt exclusionary patterns, fostering inclusion and belonging. At the leadership level, allyship involves advocating for equitable practices, while at the team level, expressing gratitude for equal opportunities is crucial. Individuals are expected to embrace a learner mindset, committing to continuous learning without seeking recognition. Aspiring allies should invest time in understanding the triumphs and struggles of underrepresented groups, fostering empathy and informed actions to support their colleagues in various aspects of their professional lives.

Empowering employee resource groups (ERGs)

ERGs, known as affinity or business resource groups, foster belonging for underrepresented employees and allies. Whether a member, executive sponsor, or ally, participation in ERGs is valuable. ERGs contribute to diversity, inclusion, and belonging strategies, supporting talent objectives, recruitment, leadership engagement, and talent development. Joining an ERG helps create a community, fostering belonging through community-building, storytelling, leadership development, and networking. ERG leaders collaborate with DIBS practitioners, offering valuable employee insights, and their contributions are recognized through financial benefits or professional development. Visibility for ERGs is crucial, and some organizations use diversity councils to partner with leadership and prioritize DIBS in decision-making. The key takeaway is that ERGs connect underrepresented groups, allowing them to share influence within the organization.

Defining underrepresented groups (URGs)

I suggest focusing on the needs of individuals historically excluded from your company or industry, often referred to as underrepresented groups (URGs). It's crucial to understand and define what URGs mean, considering both global and local contexts. Use specific, respectful language, especially when referring to particular groups such as people with disabilities or Indigenous communities. In defining URGs locally, research and collaborate with employees to understand the historical access to opportunities and which groups are not represented in your company in specific regions. Incorporating high-quality data and local voices in your DIBs approach will effectively address the needs of key underrepresented groups across your organization.

Understanding the "why" for URG programs

Most diversity, inclusion, and belonging strategies involve development programs for underrepresented groups to cultivate strong leaders. These programs, directly aligned with business strategy, offer career advancement and valuable input for meeting the expressed needs of underrepresented groups (URGs). URGs often represent an underutilized internal talent pool, as research indicates they receive less actionable feedback compared to dominant groups, hindering their growth. However, URG programs should shift from teaching assimilation to dominant characteristics and instead focus on authentic leadership, purpose, business acumen, and unwritten rules of career advancement. Embracing and appreciating differences within the organization is crucial, fostering a culture where everyone's unique attributes are accepted. Even for smaller organizations without dedicated programs, creating development opportunities for underrepresented talent aligns with business goals and contributes to broader success.

Using data to drive URG success

A robust Diversity, Inclusion, and Belonging (DIB) strategy is about expanding organizational impact and opportunities for underrepresented groups (URGs). To ensure URG programs benefit both the organization and its employees, start by gathering high-quality data on URG needs. Obtain buy-in for self-identification data while complying with privacy laws and implementing necessary protections. Clearly communicate the purpose and reassure employees that data collection aims to enhance their experience. Focus on metrics supporting compelling data stories, tracking trends across URGs through employee surveys. Evaluate comfort levels, access to quality assignments, and other relevant metrics. Identify gaps and take targeted action, showcasing success stories over time. Optimize metrics by analyzing data across multiple identity groups for more nuanced insights. Consider global differences in the employee experience and recognize that solutions should cater to everyone, including those at the intersection of multiple underrepresented groups.

URG development in practice

Companies often don't need to build development programs from scratch; nearby colleges, universities, or professional associations may offer suitable programs for a fee. Ensure that the company sponsors these efforts and avoids burdening the groups it serves. When initiating development programs, identify the specific problem to address and base decisions on inclusive perspectives and organizational data. Tailor programs to address broken rungs in the corporate ladder, such as disparities in promotion rates. Adapt programs to meet global and local needs, considering factors like higher attrition rates for certain groups. Explore vendor-created solutions when they align with the organization's goals, vetting external coaches or facilitators with samples or case studies. Stay focused on solving problems and involving people to avoid wasting time and resources. These tools will help guide the organization toward essential metrics for underrepresented group (URG) talent.

Building strong internal cross-functional partnerships

To foster belonging for all employees, it's crucial to cultivate relationships and gain support from various partners. Success in Diversity, Inclusion, and Belonging (DIBs) relies on partners advancing DIBs goals even in the absence of dedicated DIBs roles. Explore all parts of your organization for potential partnerships, mapping DIBs practices and identifying areas where your work can expand. Engage partners strategically, recognizing the impact of environmental factors and the influence of people in different functions on the employee experience. Manage relationships with internal stakeholders effectively, setting clear goals and involving the right people in discussions. Establish trust, acknowledge successes, and communicate needs to engage partners, especially those unfamiliar with inclusive practices. Building authentic relationships with key individuals is essential for navigating high and low moments that impact employees. Identify the top three internal partnerships necessary to advance DIBs goals and positively impact surrounding communities.

Building strong external partnerships

Collaborating with organizations representing underrepresented communities has provided valuable insights into different customer needs. This enables teams to develop products and services with a broader range of users in mind. The key message is that external partnerships allow teams to connect with the existing and future workforce, customers, and clients. Prioritize engagement outside your company's walls, understanding the needs and concerns of external partners. Approach these relationships with humility, curiosity, and accountability, and be open to learning from feedback.

External partnerships are essential for attracting and retaining top talent. Everyone should contribute to nurturing diverse networks, shifting focus from transactional hiring to building meaningful connections. Collaborate with external partners to ensure products serve a diverse customer base, testing accessibility and addressing cross-cultural needs. Cultivate a company culture that values and leverages external relationships for mutual benefit. With the right internal and external partnerships, your organization can provide a meaningful workplace experience and deliver excellent products and services to underrepresented communities.

Start taking action in your DEIB work today

As a starting point, focus on leading with inspiration and infusing DIBs into your current work. Consider your immediate sphere of influence and carry that energy forward. Additionally, prioritize alignment with those driving DIBs work within your organization. This alignment ensures impactful efforts. Remember, DIBs are integrated into everything you do. Your commitment extends beyond yourself; it's for the benefit of everyone in your company. Take action and apply what you've learned today.

Chapter 10 How to Achieve More by Doing Less

What does it mean to drop the task?

I used to fear dropping tasks, believing it was a failure that would disappoint everyone around me. Over time, I redefined "drop the task" as letting go of unrealistic expectations and focusing on what truly matters. We will explore how you can redefine it for yourself and create a life you're passionate about. Dropping the task means acknowledging challenges but recognizing the journey is worthwhile.

Why dropping the task is essential for leading yourself

In our busy lives, managing various tasks is crucial for personal efficiency. Dropping tasks becomes a strategy to proactively plan and regain a sense of control. Pause now and visualize what dropping tasks would mean for you— how it looks, feels, and sounds like in your life.

Why dropping the task is essential for leading others

Leadership, as defined by Marshall Ganz, is taking responsibility to help others achieve a shared purpose amid uncertainty. In challenging times with limited resources, effective leadership may require personal commitment when traditional means are unavailable. Being a trusted leader involves managing your time and energy, serving as a model for others. Establishing boundaries is crucial; a strategy for saying no involves expressing gratitude, explaining current priorities, firmly declining, and expressing appreciation. This leadership approach empowers others to articulate their boundaries and ensures collective success.

Invisible job descriptions

We are born into specific roles, such as daughter or son, and throughout life, we acquire various titles like friend, student, worker, manager, husband, or wife. Despite diverse backgrounds, cultures, and values, people share similar expectations for being "good" in these roles. For instance, being a good sister might involve responding to texts promptly, while being a good associate may require early attendance at meetings. The pressure to fulfill these invisible job descriptions is common, leading to feelings of overwhelm. Pay attention to moments of pressure tied to these expectations. The next exploration will focus on the origin of these job descriptions and how to regain control over them.

The source of your expectations

Our collective job descriptions, despite diverse backgrounds, are shaped by three shared experiences: modeling from trusted individuals during our youth, influence from popular culture, and the impact of advertising. Advertising further contributes to our expectations, bombarding us with messages about what we should aspire to be. These collective experiences shape the invisible job descriptions we feel pressured to fulfill.

Exercise: Two questions to uncover what has shaped you

To truly be in control of our lives, we must uncover the origins of our expectations. Otherwise, we're essentially living someone else's narrative—perhaps that of a trusted figure from our past, a skilled TV scriptwriter, or a savvy advertiser. Take a moment to jot down the various roles you occupy, such as being a manager or a granddaughter. For each role, consider what defines a "good" occupant of that role. Then, question how you acquired those definitions. It's essential to jot down your initial thoughts without overthinking. You might discover that your criteria for being a "good X" often trace back to external influences.

Deciding what matters most

When helping others drop the task, I often ask, "What matters most to you?" People typically mention aspects of their lives like their career or family. To go deeper, I encourage identifying what they hope to achieve in relation to these priorities. For me, three key priorities are nurturing a healthy partnership, raising conscious global citizens, and advancing humanity. If you're unsure where to begin, involve people from different contexts who've known you well. Ask for stories about when they observed you at your best. Listen, record, and identify commonalities. Another tip is self-reflection, envisioning what people would say about you at your funeral. Consider the impact you'd want to be remembered for, providing insights into what matters most to you now.

Exercise: To-do list deep dive

One major challenge is our unrealistic daily expectations. In a workshop, participants listed tasks for an ideal day, realizing they exceeded the 24-hour day. The epiphany was that the daily burden is humanly impossible. To overcome this, clarify your highest and best use, creating filters. Pause and list overwhelming tasks. Ask five questions for each: 1) Does it align with what matters most? 2) Can I do it well with little effort? 3) Is it exclusively my task? 4) Is it callous to delegate? 5) Does it bring joy? If three or more answers are "no," consider dropping the task.

Drop the task equation

To drop the task, focus daily attention on your highest and best use. Ask two key questions: Can I do it well with little effort? Is it exclusive to me? For instance, in raising conscious global citizens, I excel in guiding and encouraging others. To maintain discipline, create a fill-in-the-blank statement, like "Is [task] my highest and best use to achieve [what matters most]?" Use this daily to stay focused and make informed decisions on tasks. For example, when considering speaking at a conference, I'd ask, "Is this my highest and best use in advancing humanity?" This practice helped me discern when to say yes or delegate tasks.

Rewriting your job description

To address guilt when dropping tasks, realign your values with intentionally chosen and feasible behaviors. Rewrite your job description by reassessing expectations. For instance, as a manager, I initially associated mentorship with support but realigned to focus on giving critical feedback, saving time. Engage stakeholders, such as colleagues and family, to gather their top expectations, discovering that often, your expectations are higher than theirs, contributing to a revised job description.

Imaginary delegation

I used to engage in imaginary delegation, assuming others knew their tasks without explicit communication. This led to frustration and resentment. Imaginary delegation fails because people can't read minds. Recognizing this pattern is crucial for effective collaboration. Seeking feedback from others about any perceived pressure can increase self-awareness. The next step is learning the opposite approach, "delegating with joy," a more effective way to communicate tasks and expectations clearly.

Dropping the task at home

The practice of "delegating with joy" involves asking for help in a way that considers others' interests, inspiring their support. Implementing this at home is crucial for reducing stress and improving overall well-being, fostering a positive impact on work performance. When initiating such conversations, it's essential to communicate thoughtfully and schedule dedicated times for discussions with family members or roommates.

Dropping the task at work

Delegating with joy at work showcases self-awareness and aids in managing up. It helps managers remember assigned tasks and provides valuable support. When delegating with joy at work, begin with the company's objectives. State past success or strengths related to the goal, share challenges, and propose solutions. Seek feedback from your boss or manager. Schedule these intentional conversations in advance for a more successful and freeing work environment.

Finding your Crew

A strong crew has members from different backgrounds, provides objective perspectives, and has established accountability frameworks. Regular meetings involve updates, open-ended questions, and mutual support. As you navigate your journey, consider curating a diverse, objective, and accountable crew to ensure you're not navigating alone. Use LinkedIn or seek recommendations to find suitable crew members who can support your success.

Chapter 11 Becoming an Ally to All

Why you should care about allyship

Allyship is a powerful tool for fostering inclusivity, as small individual adjustments can lead to significant cultural changes. Just as Nobel Prize-winning economist Thomas Shelling illustrated with a board of squares, slight modifications in behavior can result in more integration. In the workplace, numerous individuals making small adjustments can profoundly impact overall culture, often being the catalyst for change. Studies indicate that allies are often more effective in addressing non-inclusive behavior and advocating for diversity, and they can significantly impact the lives of their colleagues. While being an ally is morally right, it also contributes to personal learning and growth and provides a support network when needed. Striking a middle path between fear of mistakes and uninformed action, this course equips you with the tools to act confidently as an ally.

The allyship model

The traditional view of allyship sees it as an on/off switch, but it's more beneficial to view it as an evolving journey. Researcher Keith Edwards identifies three stages: "ally to one," "ally to some," and "ally to all." Moving beyond the basic ally to one stage, ally to some involves focusing on a group, recognizing systemic issues, and acting when inspired. However, it still views oneself as an exception to the system. The goal is to reach the ally to all stage, where the focus is on everyone, including oneself. This stage involves understanding that everyone needs allies, fostering sustainable allyship practices, and seeking to improve the entire system. By viewing allyship as a journey, mistakes are seen as opportunities to learn, and a more forgiving attitude allows growth and self-compassion.

Be an ally to yourself

The Empathy Triangle is a tool for allyship involving three roles: the ally, the affected person, and the source of non-inclusive behavior. In the ally's reflection, key questions include: Are motivations genuine? Is there enough information to act? Are systemic solutions considered? And, have relationships with the affected person and source been thoughtfully assessed? Asking these questions ensures thoughtful allyship actions.

Be an ally to the affected person

Regarding your relationship with the affected person, ask, "Am I assisting them as they wish to be helped?" This emphasizes helping based on their preferences, not yours. Instead of following the golden rule (helping as you'd like to be helped), consider the platinum rule (helping as they'd like to be helped). This might involve asking if your intervention could be perceived negatively and whether you should seek permission or guidance. For example, if a colleague makes an inappropriate comment, rather than publicly addressing it, consider approaching the affected person privately, offering support, and seeking their input on the best way to address the situation. This approach respects their autonomy and allows for more effective collaboration.

Be an ally to the source of non-inclusive behavior

Regarding your relationship with the source of non-inclusive behavior, consider being an ally to them. This might seem counterintuitive, as the instinct is often to focus on supporting the affected person. However, the reason for being an ally to the source is that everyone takes turns in different roles. At some point, you may find yourself in the position of the source of non-inclusive behavior. Acknowledging this reality helps foster a culture of mutual support. Sharing a personal example, the speaker recalls a time when they unintentionally exhibited non-inclusive behavior. In response, they apologized, sought allyship from the affected individuals, and emphasized separating the behavior from the person. This approach, focusing on growth and understanding, led to a more cohesive and supportive class dynamic. It underscores the importance of having tools to navigate such situations when they arise.

Apply the empathy triangle to yourself

The Empathy Triangle guides allyship interventions by examining the ally's relationship with herself and others. In a case study, if Elizabeth, with a visual impairment, seeks directions to the cafeteria and declines your offer to accompany her, using the Empathy Triangle can provide insights. Reflect on your motivations; ensure they are geared towards creating inclusivity rather than seeking rewards. Assess your knowledge of disability issues to avoid inadvertently patronizing Elizabeth. If mistakes occur, view them as opportunities for learning. Key questions for self-reflection include having the right motivations and being adequately informed to act.

Apply the empathy triangle to an affected person

In a case study involving your role as an ally to the affected person, imagine your colleague Maria faces unconscious gender bias in a team meeting. If you're an ally to some, you might publicly confront the bias in support of women. However, considering if you're helping Maria as she wants, you might realize public advocacy could embarrass her. As an ally to all, you may wait until after the meeting to discuss support privately with Maria, seeking permission before intervening next time. When immediate action is needed, address the issue on your behalf without involving Maria, expressing concern about interruptions and suggesting a change in behavior. This case study emphasizes asking whether your assistance aligns with the affected person's preferences, guided by questions about potential unhelpfulness and the need for permission or advice.

Apply the empathy triangle to the source

In the final case study involving the ally, the affected party, and the source of non-inclusive behavior, consider a scenario where Arnold makes a biased joke about Roberto being on "Hispanic time." If you're an ally to some, you may condemn Arnold to protect Roberto. However, if you ask whether you're being an ally to the source, you could approach Arnold without labeling him as a bad person. Instead, inquire about his intent, explain the negative impact of ethnic stereotypes, and share your own learning experiences. This case study underscores the importance of being an ally to the source of non-inclusive behavior and emphasizes that being an ally to all means being an adversary to none.

Take allyship forward

In summary, effective allyship involves three key steps. First, understand the three-stage allyship model. Second, utilize the Empathy Triangle to reflect on your role, support the affected person as they wish to be helped, and be an ally to the source of non-inclusive behavior. Finally, actively engage in allyship, progressing from ally to one, through ally to some, towards ally to all behaviors While allyship may seem daunting, liken it to learning a language where mistakes are part of the process. Encourage those striving to be allies, and may your allyship journey bring success as we collectively become better allies to all

Chapter 12 Building a Data-Driven Skills-First Workforce Strategy

The role of uncertainty in skills

The COVID-19 pandemic has triggered significant organizational changes, prompting a reevaluation of strategies. During uncertain times, understanding the workforce's skills composition becomes crucial for companies undergoing transformations. For instance, when entering new markets, knowing employees language skills is essential. This knowledge guides decisions between buying talent and building it in-house. Assessing existing skills can also aid in optimizing talent during changes in business focus, preventing unnecessary layoffs.

How to translate business strategy to skills

Translating business strategy into skills is a manageable process when broken down into key steps. Step one involves focusing on impactful areas that drive profit or revenue, anticipating future organizational needs. Step two is to clarify current roles and skills, for instance, identifying critical skills for a solutions architect in a cloud-focused priority. Step three entails mapping out future roles and skills, addressing any skill gaps through hiring or training. Step four involves creating action plans to close skill gaps, considering upskilling existing employees and external hiring. This systematic approach simplifies the process of aligning skills with business strategy.

What skills are required of everyone in the future

According to the World Economic Forum, skills have a short shelf life, with technical skills lasting around two and a half years. To stay relevant, continuous re-skilling is necessary. The Future of Jobs report estimates that 44% of workers' core skills will change between 2023 and 2027, emphasizing the need for preparation. Fast-growing jobs include AI and machine learning specialists, sustainability specialists, and business intelligence analysts. In-demand skills include creative thinking, analytical thinking, technological literacy, curiosity, resilience, flexibility, agility, systems thinking, AI and big data, motivation, self-awareness, talent management, service orientation, and customer service. Creating a training and development plan for organizations involves searching for relevant courses in learning management systems.

How can skills improve diversity, equity, and inclusion?

Many large organizations have shifted to skills-based hiring to enhance diversity representation. The rise of coding boot camps and online learning resources has made skills more accessible, prompting companies to reconsider degree requirements. By focusing on skills, companies can attract candidates capable of performing well, irrespective of degree status, thereby expanding the talent pool. This shift is particularly beneficial for diversity, as it addresses disparities in educational attainment among different ethnic and racial groups. The strategy extends beyond hiring, as leveraging skills data for internal roles can enhance the retention and engagement of employees from underrepresented backgrounds. Skills data can also help mitigate biases in promotions and internal opportunities, providing visibility to all candidates with the necessary skills.

What is a skill?

A skill is the application of knowledge for measurable business outcomes, distinct from competency, which encompasses specific knowledge, behaviors, attitudes, and skills applied in task execution. Skills are fundamental components of competencies. However, confusion arises when the same term is used for both skills and competencies. While skills are often transferable, competencies are context-specific, reflecting their application within a particular company or role. For instance, strategic planning is a competency covering skills like deductive reasoning, but the specific knowledge and contacts for strategic planners in manufacturing differ from those in professional services. Unlike skills, company-specific competencies are not typically included on resumes, which focus on transferable skills.

How to choose a skills architecture

Skills architecture is the organized structure of skills that enhances visibility into employees' execution of business capabilities. Two common approaches to defining relationships within skills architecture are taxonomy and ontology. A taxonomy organizes skills hierarchically, categorizing essential skills for the business, providing clarity and fixed development paths. On the other hand, ontology identifies and distinguishes concepts and relationships, offering flexibility for evolving meanings over time. While a taxonomy is more structured and suitable for static skills, an ontology is dynamic and adapts to changes, providing context across domains. The choice between them is strategic, dependent on company culture, openness to change, and how the organization intends to use skills data. AI tools can expedite the utilization of skills in workforce strategy, suggesting skills based on employees' experiences and job history. The decision between taxonomy and ontology involves strategic considerations rather than purely technical factors.

How to capture and validate skills

One common query is how to manage and update skills data effectively. While using spreadsheets is possible, it can lead to issues like inconsistent data entry, version control problems, and difficulty linking data to other employee details. Storing skills in an Human Resource Information System (HRIS) or Human Capital Management (HCM) system is preferable for easier analysis and integration with other data points. Another question is how to validate skills. Options include self-reporting, manager or Subject Matter Expert (SME) sign-off, or a hybrid approach. The decision depends on the need for data trustworthiness and the simplicity of the validation process. For safety-critical skills, expert validation may be essential, while for non-regulatory skills, self-reporting can be more straightforward. Assessments can also be used, but the choice should balance buy-in ease with process complexity.

How to store skills data

Once you've captured and validated skills data, determining where to store it depends on various factors. If you want to track skill proficiency across different roles, an HCM or HRIS system may be more suitable than a Learning Management Systems (LMS), which often lacks detailed job history information. The choice between systems is a talent strategy decision aligned by the senior leadership team. Skills can be included in performance management processes or kept on employee profiles without a performance connection. While using Excel to start is acceptable, it has drawbacks such as inconsistency, version control issues, and privacy concerns. Migrating to a more robust system is advisable. Compliance with data privacy regulations and potential opt-ins for performance use should be considered. In organizations with taxonomies, correct skill capture is crucial, limiting certain skills to specific roles. Ontologies offer more flexibility in data entry but involve strategic, not just technical, decisions. Some organizations may explore AI for data entry assistance or skill suggestions, impacting future AI tool utilization.

How to update skills data regularly

If you use an HCM or HRIS, establish a periodic review process, recommended at least once a year. For efficiency, consider quarterly reviews tied to career conversations. Events like promotions or job changes can trigger additional reviews. However, gaining organizational buy-in for the importance of accurate data is essential, ensuring employees see value in the process. When dealing with emerging skills not yet in any system, configure the system to allow employees to enter such skills as free-form text, eventually grouping and potentially adding them to the existing skills taxonomy.

Avoid common pitfalls

Why do many organizations lack up-to-date employee skills data, despite its importance? Common pitfalls include an obsession with perfection over progress, spending excessive time debating nuances. Using a pre-existing skills taxonomy as a starting point can be more efficient. Unclear ownership hampers progress, with various departments vying for control. The solution involves empowering any combination of relevant COEs with a clear leader serving as a tie-breaker. Non-repeatable processes, especially complex ones, hinder regular updates. Simplifying and incorporating AI can expedite the skills data entry process.

Getting it right

Follow these four steps to initiate a successful skills-based workforce strategy. First, identify a clear business problem with top or bottom-line impact that senior leaders support solving. Ensure the problem aligns with business objectives, not just HR concerns. Second, secure buy-in from employees and managers for the data-gathering process by articulating clear benefits. Define what's in it for them, emphasizing opportunities for development, promotions, or pay increases. Third, obtain manager buy-in for skill validation and data usage. Decide whether employees or managers will assess skills, considering the type of skills involved. Set clear expectations for data use, emphasizing its role in development, not compensation decisions. Fourth, analyze the collected data to identify and address skill gaps. Determine whether to hire or develop skills, adopting a buy-versus-build strategy based on urgency and internal capabilities.

How to use the data you collected

After implementing a system to collect employee skills data, consider how to leverage this information for strategic workforce planning. For instance, if your organization's upcoming product launch requires a shift in the ratio of front-end to back-end developers, analyze existing skill sets. Determine whether back-end developers can be quickly upskilled for front-end tasks. If achievable in a few months, organize training to meet the new skill ratio. However, if upskilling takes longer, consider potential layoffs, accounting for voluntary attrition rates to avoid excessive terminations. Assess the overlap of skills between roles to gauge the feasibility of temporary reassignments. Utilize tools like LinkedIn's economic graph drop transition tool for insights and consider the extent of skill match scores for successful reassignments or upskilling strategies.